W9-BCO-160

PRESCOTT PUBLIC LIBRARY
LIBRARY
PRESCOTT, WI 54021

Imitating *Nature*

From **Fish Gills** to Underwater Breathing

Imitating *Nature*

From Fish Gills to Underwater Breathing

Toney Allman

KIDHAVEN PRESS

An imprint of Thomson Gale, a part of The Thomson Corporation

THOMSON

GALE ™

Detroit • New York • San Francisco • San Diego • New Haven, Conn. • Waterville, Maine • London • Munich

© 2007 Thomson Gale, a part of The Thomson Corporation.

Thomson and Star Logo are trademarks and Gale and KidHaven Press are registered trademarks used herein under license.

For more information, contact
KidHaven Press
27500 Drake Rd.
Farmington Hills, MI 48331-3535
Or you can visit our Internet site at http://www.gale.com

ALL RIGHTS RESERVED.
No part of this work covered by the copyright herein may be reproduced or used in any form or by any means—graphic, electronic, or mechanical, including photocopying, recording, taping, Web distribution or information storage retrieval systems—without the written permission of the publisher.

Every effort has been made to trace the owners of copyrighted material.

LIBRARY OF CONGRESS CATALOGING-IN-PUBLICATION DATA

Allman, Toney.
  From fish gills to underwater breathing / by Toney Allman.
      p. cm. — (Imitating nature)
  Includes bibliographical references and index.
  ISBN 0-7377-3608-9 (hard cover : alk. paper) 1. Underwater breathing apparatus—
      Juvenile literature. 2. Gills—Juvenile literature. 3. Imitation—Juvenile literature.
      I. Title. II. Series.
  VM984.A45 2006
  627'.72—dc22
                                                              2006004550

Printed in The United States of America

Contents

CHAPTER 1

A Breath of Water

On a summer day in 2000, in Zichron Yaakov, Israel, seven-year-old Aviv Bodner asked his father why people could not breathe underwater without oxygen tanks. His father, Alan Bodner, is an engineer, a person who uses science and math to solve problems and build new inventions. Instead of dismissing Aviv's question, Bodner started imagining the possibilities. People have often dreamed of being able to breathe in oceans and rivers without the need of heavy **scuba** gear. Bodner wondered if he could invent something to make the dream come true. What if people could breathe underwater like fish?

Air Is There

Fish need oxygen to survive, just as humans do, but the air they breathe is in the water where they live. The air is dissolved in oceans, rivers, and lakes, just as sugar dissolves in water. There is not nearly as much

Engineer Alan Bodner wondered if people could somehow breathe underwater like fish.

oxygen in water as there is in the air that people breathe. Only about 2 percent of ocean water, for example, is dissolved air, and only about a third of that air is oxygen. Air in Earth's atmosphere is made up of 21 percent oxygen, thirty times more than seawater. Nevertheless, fish are able to breathe in plenty of oxygen to meet their needs.

Gills, Not Lungs

Instead of using lungs for breathing, as humans do, fish breathe in oxygen with systems called **gills**. When people breathe, they pull air into their lungs. There, blood pumped by the heart picks up the oxygen in the air and carries it throughout the body. In a similar way, gills filter air and oxygen from water.

Just a Tad

In general, every quart (1 liter) of water contains only 1 teaspoon (5ml) of dissolved oxygen.

Gills are the slits on either side of the fish's head. They open into the inside of the fish's throat. Each gill is made of a stiff arch where many feathery structures called **filaments** are attached. These filaments have millions of folds in them called **lamellae**. Tiny blood vessels called **capillaries** run through the lamellae, bringing blood that is low in oxygen to the gills. When water flows through the gills, it flows across

Gills are the two slits on a fish's head that open into its throat.

the capillaries. Because the oxygen in the blood is low compared to the oxygen in the water, oxygen naturally seeps into the capillaries. Then, as the fish's heart pumps, the blood vessels carry oxygen-rich blood throughout the fish's body.

Inside each gill, feathery filaments attach to a stiff arch.

How Fish Gills Work

Fish extract oxygen from the water around them. In order to do this, most fish must open and close their mouths to pump water through their gills.

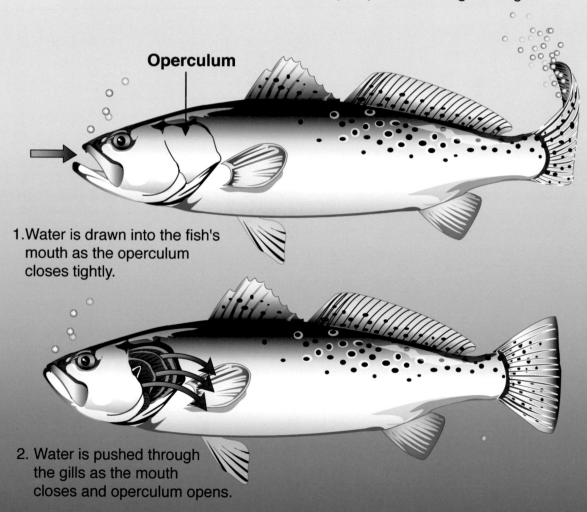

Operculum

1. Water is drawn into the fish's mouth as the operculum closes tightly.

2. Water is pushed through the gills as the mouth closes and operculum opens.

Glub, Glub

Most fish have to pump water through their gills to get oxygen. They open and shut their mouths to pump water across their gills. When a fish opens its mouth, the outside covering on its gills, called the **operculum**, shuts up tightly, so water is drawn into the fish's mouth. When the fish closes its mouth, the operculum opens, and water rushes through the gills and back out into the water. Over and over, the fish opens and shuts its mouth, and each time, oxygen passes from the fresh water into the fish's blood.

Some fish, such as tuna, cannot pump water through their gills. Instead, these fish must swim continually so they can breathe. As it swims, a tuna keeps its mouth open so that water can flow through its mouth and pass over its gills. If the fish stopped swimming, it would suffocate. As long as water is flowing through the gills, however, the fish filters oxygen and stays alive and healthy.

Fishy Thinking

Bodner asked himself why people could not do the same thing. He could not give people actual gills, but

Gill Power

Because there is so little air in water, fish gills must work extremely efficiently. If people were breathing water like fish, they would have to take 450 breaths each minute just to get enough oxygen to survive.

Some fish, like this tuna, must swim constantly in order to breathe properly.

perhaps he could invent a wearable breathing device that worked like gills. It would filter out the dissolved air in water, and people could breathe its oxygen, just as fish do. Bodner decided to try to build just such an invention.

CHAPTER 2

Like a Fish

In 2001, Bodner started his own company, Like-A-Fish Technologies. He set to work on inventing an underwater breathing system that would operate differently than the air tanks used today.

Better than Air Tanks

Divers carry tanks of compressed air with them for breathing underwater. So do any submarines that do not use nuclear power. These tanks must be refilled at air stations whenever the air is running low. Divers breathe in air from their tanks and then breathe out the bad air, which is full of carbon dioxide, back into the water. Nonnuclear submarines do much the same thing. The air is pumped into living quarters from the tanks, and the bad air people breathe out is

Alan Bodner explains the Like-A-Fish Technologies underwater breathing system to a reporter.

cleaned from the submarine with an air-scrubbing device.

Bodner's invention would make air tanks unnecessary. It would filter air from water so that divers and submarines would not have to carry air tanks. They would just carry a device that extracts air from the water. The device could be worn on a lightweight vest or attached to the submarine.

Bodner's proposed underwater breathing system would make heavy air tanks (inset and on diver's back) unnecessary for diving.

Air out of Water

In 2003, Bodner succeeded in developing a laboratory model of a tankless breathing device that imitates fish gills. The model filters air from water in an aquarium in the laboratory, just as gills do. It operates with a pump that runs on batteries and pulls in water. Next, the water is pumped through a hose into an air separator. The air separator is a **centrifuge**, which is a machine that spins very fast. It spins so fast that the air cannot stay dissolved in the water. It is released from the water as a gas. Then, the air floats into an air bag, or balloon, that can be connected to a breathing hose for a person.

Improving the System

Bodner's laboratory model worked well, but it was not yet practical for people or submarines. It needed to pump hundreds of gallons of water every minute to filter enough air out of water for people to breathe. That would require a battery weighing 100 pounds (45kg) to run the pump and air separator! No diver could wear anything so heavy. Bodner had to figure out a way to use fewer gallons of water.

Nuclear Submarines

Nuclear submarines do not need to carry tanks of compressed air. They actually separate oxygen from water molecules so crews can breathe. This chemical process works well, but it is very complicated, extremely expensive, and takes a huge amount of power. It is a much different system than Bodner's, which simply filters the dissolved air from water instead of changing the water itself.

He decided to try to use the same filtered air over and over but scrub out the bad air. The bad air has too much carbon dioxide in it for people to breathe, but it still has plenty of leftover oxygen in it, too. Bodner wanted to reuse this air so that the pump did not have to take in so many gallons of

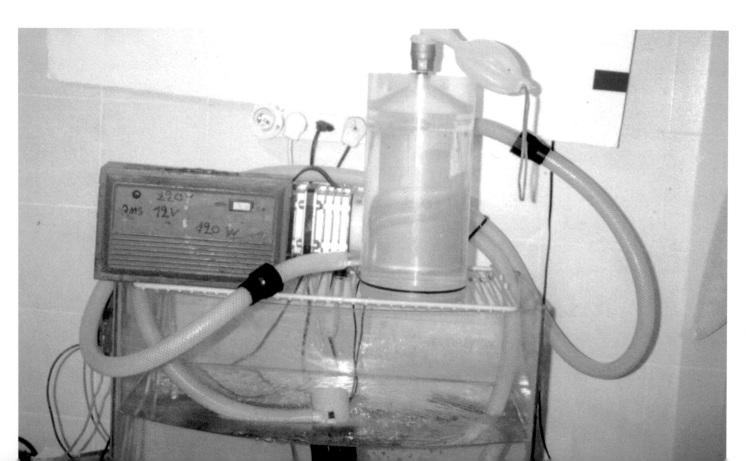

A successful laboratory model of Bodner's breathing device (shown) was developed in 2003.

Oceans Are Like Sodas

Carbonated sodas are fizzy because they contain dissolved gas—carbon dioxide. Sodas stay fizzy until they are opened because they are under pressure inside soda cans. When a soda can is popped open, the pressure is released, and that is why the soda fizzes. Some of the carbon dioxide escapes because the pressure is lowered when the can is opened. A centrifuge does the same thing to seawater. By rapidly rotating, it lowers the pressure in the water, and the air is released as a gas.

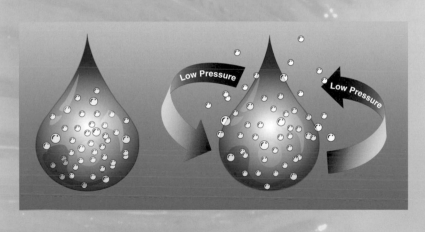

fresh water each minute to make fresh air in the separator. A diver could breathe out the bad air back into the air bag instead of into the water and breathe the air in again when it was scrubbed clean of carbon dioxide.

Bodner attached an air scrubber to his invention, like the kind submarines use. It made the used air fit for humans to breathe. An air scrubber is expensive and very difficult to build, but it makes the underwater breathing device more efficient. It needs to take in only 53 gallons (200 liters) of water per minute. A battery to run this system could weigh just 2 pounds (1kg) and still filter an hour's worth of air to breathe before the battery ran out of power.

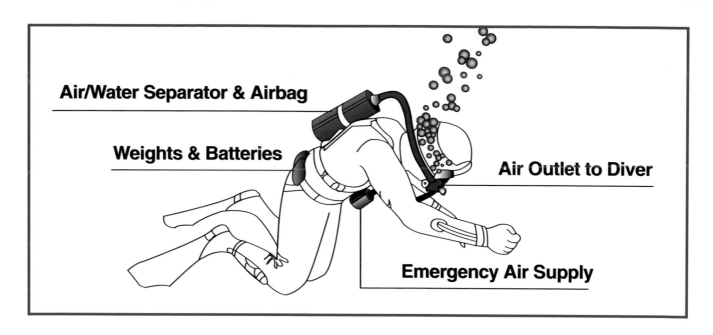

Air/Water Separator & Airbag

Weights & Batteries

Air Outlet to Diver

Emergency Air Supply

Yes, It Works

With the air scrubber, Bodner decided his invention was practical. He wanted to build a **prototype**, a first working example, of his system. He got patents for the invention in Europe and in the United States. (The patent was proof that he had designed the device. It meant that no one could steal his idea.) Bodner was ready to turn his laboratory model into a real breathing system for people.

CHAPTER 3

Future Visions

Bodner is a scuba diver himself and knows how valuable being able to breathe like a fish would be. He hopes to build his lightweight vest for divers in the near future, but his first breathing system prototype will be for an underwater **habitat**, or livable structure. Once the prototype is successful in a habitat, he can work on figuring out long-lasting batteries and power sources that will make people comfortable underwater as never before.

The BioSUB

First, Bodner plans to help one man live independently underwater. In 2006, Like-A-Fish Technologies agreed to build an underwater breathing system for a single-person habitat in Australia. It is named BioSUB, and the man who will live in it is Lloyd Godson. Godson is a diver and

A longtime scuba diver, Alan Bodner knows how valuable a lightweight underwater breathing system would be.

scientist who wants to prove that a person can survive underwater without help from the outside world. Bodner will make it possible for Godson to breathe in his underwater home.

BioSUB is supported by the Australian Geographic Society, which gave $50,000 for building the underwater habitat. It will be a living place made of two large, metal shipping containers that have been welded together. It will be sunk into a deep freshwater lake formed in an old Australian gravel quarry. The lake is called The Pit and is 52 feet (16m) deep. It is often used for scientific experiments. Under the surface of the lake, Godson will eat, sleep, and grow his own food. He will recycle all his trash and waste. He will get the electricity to power the habitat from the energy of the Sun. His only communication with the outside world will be with a high-speed Internet connection.

Bodner poses with BioSUB scientist Lloyd Godson (left) while in Greece.

From Fish Gills to Underwater Breathing

Bodner's system that filters air from water as fish gills do will be attached to the habitat. It will extract oxygen from water for Godson to breathe. Sometime in 2006, Bodner's prototype will be installed in Bio-SUB, but the underwater breathing system will not

Lloyd Godson stands inside one of the large, metal shipping containers from the BioSUB project.

In Harmony with Nature

Lloyd Godson is determined that BioSUB will get along with all the other life in The Pit. The Pit is home to several kinds of fish, underwater plants, turtles, freshwater shrimp, and many insects. Godson will not throw any trash or waste into the water. He will recycle and reuse his garbage and human waste by putting it through a cleaning system and then using it as fertilizer for the plants he grows.

run on its own batteries yet. Instead, it will plug into the power that is running the habitat. That is because a person living underwater 24 hours a day, day after day, must have huge amounts of air. Enormous amounts of water will have to be filtered to keep Godson alive and comfortable, and that requires a large amount of power for the pump and air separator.

Divers and Submarines

Once the prototype for BioSUB is working successfully, however, Bodner plans to return to his efforts to design a lightweight underwater breathing vest for divers. He hopes to provide the vest with a battery like those in cell phones or laptop computers. When that time comes, divers will be able to move effortlessly underwater and will not have to worry about refilling oxygen tanks regularly. They will swim underwater like fish, limited only by the life of their batteries.

Bodner believes that his breathing system can be used in small submarines, too. The Israeli navy has already met with him to discuss building his underwater breathing system for some of their submarines.

Breathing Cities

Someday, Like-A-Fish breathing systems might even be built in a size that could support an underwater city of people. Bodner imagines how much bigger a habitat could be if a large underwater breathing system

The Israeli navy is working with Bodner to create an underwater breathing system for their submarines.

based on fish gills were available. He says there could be a whole city of people under a huge glass dome. The city's residents would breathe air filtered directly from the ocean water, and the air would never run out. Perhaps the day will come when people can live per-

Alan Bodner believes his underwater breathing system may someday make an undersea city possible.

Habitat for Rent

Jules' Undersea Lodge is a hotel for scuba divers off Key Largo, Florida. Guests dive into an entrance in the habitat and then stay in a luxury underwater environment where they can sleep in private rooms, visit the dining room, watch movies, and look out 42-inch (107cm) round windows at underwater views. People can even have weddings at the lodge. The unusual hotel uses compressed air tanks and is very expensive to visit. Someday such hotels may get air directly from seawater and become common vacation places.

manently in underwater cities that take air from the water, as fish gills do.

Dreams of Gills

No one knows if Bodner's vision for the future will come true. Many people, however, share his dream and enthusiastically await the time when humans can breathe underwater like fish.

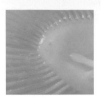

Glossary

capillaries: Tiny blood vessels that exchange substances such as oxygen and carbon dioxide between blood and body tissues.

centrifuge: A device that rotates around a central axis and spins materials in order to separate out dissolved particles or to separate different materials from one another.

filaments: Fine, threadlike body structures; the feathery structures of fish gills.

gills: The breathing organs of fish and other aquatic animals that filter oxygen from water.

habitat: A dwelling that provides a controlled environment in places where a human could not ordinarily survive, such as underwater or in outer space.

lamellae (luh-MEL-ee): Thin scales, folds, plates, or layers in tissue. *Lamellae* is plural, and *lamella* (luh-MEL-uh) is singular, for one fold.

operculum (oh-PURK-yuh-lum): A lid or flap over an opening, such as the covering of a gill.

prototype: The first working model of an invention.

scuba: An acronym for "self-contained underwater breathing apparatus"—the compressed air tanks and breathing hose that divers use to breathe under the water.

# For Further Exploration

Books

Eyewitness Guides, *Fish*. New York: DK, 2005. Learn about all kinds of fish—where they live, how they live, and the weird and wonderful habits they have.

————, *Shark*. New York: DK, 2004. Read about the fascinating but dangerous predators of the sea. Many kinds of sharks are described, and their importance in the ecosystem is explained. Learn why sharks never sleep and how they breathe.

Bruce LaFontaine, *Submarines and Underwater Exploration*. Mineola, NY: Dover, 1999. This is an amazing coloring book with 44 illustrations to color that detail human efforts to explore the depths of the oceans. There are informational captions for the pictures of submersible vessels, deep-sea scuba divers, and nuclear submarines. Even a depth chart is included.

Web Sites

The BioSUB Project (www.biosub.com.au/). This is the official BioSUB Web site. See photos of Lloyd Godson and his team preparing for the adventure, read about the history and plans for the project, and follow BioSUB's progress through Godson's online journal.

Fishes, Yahooligans! Animals (http://yahooligans.yahoo.com/content/animals/fishes/). This large Web site invites visitors to discover the lives of all sorts of sea creatures. Learn how the fish live, move, eat, and breathe, and see many photographs of some amazing fish.

How SCUBA Works, HowStuffWorks (http://entertainment.howstuffworks.com/scuba.htm). Discover how scuba divers function underwater and how their equipment keeps them alive today. Learn about the dangers of scuba diving and how divers train to become expert explorers.

Like-A-Fish Technologies (www.likeafish.biz/). This is the official Web site for Like-A-Fish Technologies.

The project status is updated regularly as progress is made with the underwater breathing system.

NOAA's Aquarius (www.uncw.edu/aquarius/). Bio-SUB is not the only underwater habitat. Aquarius is an inner-space station off the coast of Florida with a scientific laboratory where scientists complete ten-day underwater missions. Take a virtual tour of the oceanic lab and find out what scientists have learned about life under the sea.

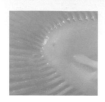

Index

Picture Credits

Cover: (From left to right) © Stephen Frink/zefa/CORBIS;
  © Ron Boardman; Frank Lane Picture Agency/CORBIS;
  © Guy Barnes; Maury Aaseng
© Bill Curtsinger/National Geographic/Getty Images, 12
© AFP/Getty Images, 23
© Guy Barness, 16
© Carolina Sarasiti, 20, 21
Maury Aaseng, 10, 17, 18, 24
© Pete Atkinson/The Image Bank/Getty Images, 14 (main)
© Ron Boardman; Frank Lane Picture Agency/CORBIS, 9
© Royalty-Free/CORBIS, 14 (inset)
© RTVi, 13, 19
© Sol R. Bodner, 7
© Stephen Frink/zefa/CORBIS, 8

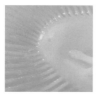

About the Author

Toney Allman has degrees from Ohio State University and the University of Hawaii. She currently lives in Virginia by the Chesapeake Bay and gets to see lots of fish.

PRESCOTT PUBLIC LIBRARY

LIBRARY

PRESCOTT, WI 54021